Writers Who Changed the World

JOHN STEINBECK

Anita Croy

LUCENT PRESS

Published in 2020 by
Lucent Press, an Imprint of Greenhaven Publishing, LLC
353 3rd Avenue
Suite 255
New York, NY 10010

Produced for Lucent by Calcium
Editors: Sarah Eason and Tim Cooke
Designers: Paul Myerscough and Lynne Lennon
Picture researcher: Rachel Blount

Picture credits: Cover: Shutterstock: Vlada Young; Inside: Library of Congress: Currier & Ives: p. 36; Federal Security Agency: p. 47; Carol M. Highsmith: p. 61; Dorothea Lange: p. 28; Russell Lee: pp. 22, 26, 29, 44; NYWT&S staff photo: p. 34; Shutterstock: Richard Cavalleri: p. 21; Tony Craddock: p. 9; ESB Professional: p. 39; Everett Historical: pp. 8, 31b, 38, 48; Sheila Fitzgerald: p. 57; Eric Isselee: p. 35; Jejim: p. 24; JLSnader: p. 32; Kit Leong: p. 58; David Litman: pp. 7, 45; Ognennaja: p. 59; Rolf_52: p. 41; Rook76: p. 52; Richard Thornton: p. 56; Wikimedia Commons: Amadscientist: p. 10; Elias Goldensky: p. 16; Dorothea Lange: pp. 12, 20, 31t; Dorothea Lange; Restored by Adam Cuerden: p. 15; Edwin Locke, for the Farm Security Administration/Office of War Information/Office of Emergency Management/Resettlement Administration: p. 50; LordHarris: p. 55; McFadden Publications, Inc.: p. 4; Mark Miller: p. 11; Naotake Murayama: p. 6; Alexander Nasmyth: p. 27; OSU Special Collections & Archives; Gerald W. Williams Collection: p. 17; Rondal Partridge/Farm Security Administration: p. 51b; Arthur Rothstein, for the Farm Security Administration: p. 19; Social Security Online: p. 37; Traveljournalist: p. 49; Unknown: pp. 14, 40, 42, 51t; USDA: p. 25; U.S. Navy, Office of Public Relations: p. 46; Works Progress Administration, Federal Art Project; Albert M. Bender, designer: p. 18.

Cataloging-in-Publication Data

Names: Croy, Anita.
Title: John Steinbeck / Anita Croy.
Description: New York : Lucent Press, 2020. | Series: Writers who changed the world | Includes glossary and index.
Identifiers: ISBN 9781534565937 (pbk.) | ISBN 9781534565944 (library bound) | ISBN 9781534565951 (ebook)
Subjects: LCSH: Steinbeck, John, 1902-1968--Juvenile literature. | Authors, American--20th century--Biography--Juvenile literature.
Classification: LCC PS3537.C79 2020 | DDC 813'.52 B--dc23

Printed in the United States of America

CPSIA compliance information: Batch #BS19KL: For further information contact Greenhaven Publishing LLC, New York, New York at 1-844-317-7404.

Please visit our website, www.greenhavenpublishing.com. For a free color catalog of all our high-quality books, call toll free 1-844-317-7404 or fax 1-844-317-7405.

CONTENTS

CHAPTER 1

This is a photograph of John Steinbeck in 1939.

JOHN STEINBECK
Biography

Born: February 27, 1902

Place of birth: Salinas, California

Mother: Olive Hamilton Steinbeck

Father: John Ernst Steinbeck

Famous for: Writing some of the most important books in American literature, such as *Of Mice and Men*, *The Grapes of Wrath*, and *East of Eden*.

How he changed the world: John Steinbeck's description of the suffering of ordinary Americans during the Great Depression of the 1930s and of the tough lives of migrant workers added greatly to the understanding of American life.

John Steinbeck's writing SHOWS the WORLD what it was like to SUFFER poverty during the Great Depression with no HOPE of a better FUTURE.

John Steinbeck

CALIFORNIAN UPBRINGING

John Steinbeck grew up in the Salinas Valley, close to the Pacific Ocean in California. The area was known for its fertile land and its large farms. After a happy childhood, in 1919 Steinbeck went to Stanford University to study literature. He quit without finishing his degree. He moved to New York City but got homesick and returned to California.

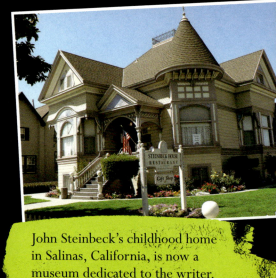

John Steinbeck's childhood home in Salinas, California, is now a museum dedicated to the writer.

While he was at Stanford, Steinbeck earned money by working as a manual laborer on farms. His experiences would later find their way into his novels. The people he met on the farms were far removed from his own comfortable life. The workers had no one to help them. If they lost their jobs, they had no way to feed themselves or their families.

His experiences would later find their way into his novels.

The Great Depression began in 1929. The U.S. economy stalled and many workers lost their jobs. Many thousands of farmers traveled across the country to California to try to make a living. There was not enough work for all of them. These were desperate times.

Words that changed the world

In Of Mice and Men, *the stable hand Crooks describes hundreds of men who come to work on the ranches, all hoping to own a small piece of land. And not a single one of them ever achieves their dream.*

Exploring the text

Crooks remarks on the hopes that attracted workers to California. They all want to buy their own piece of land. Steinbeck had met many workers dreaming of earning enough to buy their own farm. Every time, they were disappointed. The Salinas Valley and other farmland in California were owned by large companies. The people who worked in the fields could never earn enough to buy land of their own.

The Salinas Valley is still one of the most important areas of farmland in California.

HISTORY'S STORY

California grows more than 200 different types of crops. Farm owners have always used temporary workers to pick fruit and vegetables at harvest time. These migrant workers came from Mexico as well as from other parts of the country. They were only paid for the time they worked. Once the harvest was finished, they were let go.

STRUGGLING TO GET BY

This photograph shows migrant workers harvesting carrots on a farm in California in 1937.

The time Steinbeck spent in New York City was a struggle. He missed California, and he was poor. After he returned to California, Steinbeck moved to Lake Tahoe. He worked as a caretaker on an estate and then at a fish farm. While he did his day job, he wrote whenever he could. He had wanted to be a writer since he was 14 years old. In 1929, he published his first novel, *Cup of Gold*. The book told the story of the pirate Henry Morgan. It did not sell well.

A dedicated supporter

Steinbeck continued to write. He was helped by his first wife, Carol Henning, whom he married in January 1930. The couple moved around from San Francisco to Los Angeles before eventually settling in central California. Carol was very supportive of Steinbeck. She believed her husband was a great writer, and she worked a number of jobs to support them both while he wrote.

To save money, the couple lived in Steinbeck's family's summer cottage outside Monterey. Steinbeck's father also supported his son's goals, supplying him with paper to write on and lending him money. But the young couple still struggled. Despite the support of his family, Steinbeck had one failed novel to his name and no income.

A tough start

Between 1930 and 1935, Steinbeck published two more novels, *The Red Pony* and *To a God Unknown*, and a collection of short stories. The stories showed not only his love for California but also his understanding of the people who lived and worked there. Despite his talent, Steinbeck's books did not really sell and he and Carol remained poor. During the Great Depression, Steinbeck fished and grew his own vegetables, but the couple still often went hungry. They had to accept welfare to survive and even stole food from the local market. Everyone was in the same position, so the Steinbecks shared whatever they had with their friends and their friends did the same.

The big breakthrough came in 1935 when Steinbeck published *Tortilla Flat*. This humorous account of Mexican workers became a best seller. It was later turned into a successful movie.

This monument to John Steinbeck in Monterey depicts characters from his novel *Cannery Row*.

AN INFLUENTIAL FRIEND

In late 1930, Steinbeck met a man who would have a great influence on his way of thinking. Ed Ricketts was a marine biologist who was one of the first people to study ecology. Ecologists study how individual creatures interact with one another and with their whole environment. Ricketts's book, *Between Pacific Tides* (1939), looked at how whole ecosystems interact in marine environments. It is still studied by marine biologists today. Ricketts believed that humans were just one more part of a vast system that connected all living things.

This statue in Monterey remembers Steinbeck's friend Ed Ricketts.

Character inspiration

Carol worked in Ricketts's laboratory for a couple of years. Her husband and Ricketts became great friends. Steinbeck spent time in the lab learning about marine biology. Ricketts provided marine specimens for schools and colleges, and Steinbeck learned how to preserve specimens. When the lab burned down in 1936, Steinbeck helped pay for its repair. He became a partner in the business. Ricketts became a celebrity in 1945, when Steinbeck published his novel *Cannery Row*. The character of Doc in the book was modeled on Ricketts, who had to get used to people knocking on his lab door wanting to meet "Doc."

Ricketts was one of the first people to predict the dangers of overfishing, or taking too many fish from the sea. He studied sardines, which played a key role in the success of the Californian fishing industry. Between 1936 and 1937, fishers in Monterey caught 726,000 tons of sardines. By 1945, the sardine population was declining. When Ricketts was asked where all the sardines had gone, he replied, "They're in cans."

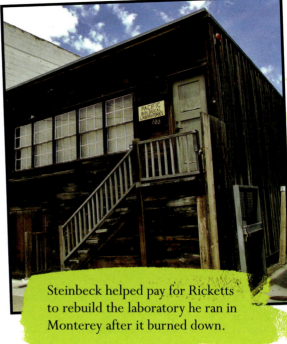

Steinbeck helped pay for Ricketts to rebuild the laboratory he ran in Monterey after it burned down.

An ocean adventure

In 1940, Steinbeck and Ricketts decided to sail around the Gulf of California to collect marine specimens. They spent six weeks sailing around and the adventure was turned into a book, *The Log from the Sea of Cortez*. Steinbeck wrote the story of their adventure, while Ricketts wrote scientific details of their discoveries. Ricketts died following a car accident in 1948. His early death robbed Steinbeck of a friend and mentor.

HISTORY'S STORY

Steinbeck wrote about Monterey's fishing industry, which was based on a street named Ocean View Avenue, in his hugely successful 1945 novel *Cannery Row*. Canneries were factories where fish were packed into cans. The book was so influential that Ocean View Avenue was renamed Cannery Row.

CHAPTER 2

This photograph shows a poor farming family in Oklahoma.

THE GREAT DEPRESSION
Background

Definition: A period when trade slowed around the world and businesses could not sell their goods. Millions of people lost their jobs.

Started: October 29, 1929

Worst period: 1932–1933

Lasted until: The start of World War II in 1939

Presidents:
Herbert Hoover (1929–1933)
Franklin D. Roosevelt (1933–1944)

Peak number of unemployed:
12–15 million people (one-quarter of the U.S. population)

Steinbeck's writing describes the TRUE HORROR of the Great Depression in the United States. He depicts a time of complete DESPAIR and DESPERATION in which every individual STRUGGLES to SURVIVE.

AMERICA GOES BUST

After World War I (1914–1918), the U.S. economy began a long boom. Most people had jobs and prices were stable. People bought modern goods that had once been seen as luxuries, such as radios and washing machines. Across the country, new skyscrapers rose above cities and roads were built as more people bought automobiles. People also invested. They bought shares in companies on the stock market, hoping they would be able to sell the shares for more money later.

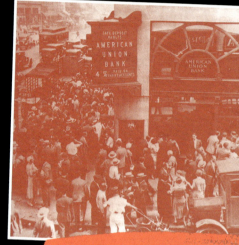

New Yorkers gather to try to take their money out of a bank before it fails.

They bought shares in companies on the stock market …

Stock market crash

The stock market grew throughout the 1920s. It seemed the boom would continue forever. Then confidence suddenly disappeared. People rushed to take their money out of the stock market, which crashed. Investments lost their value, leaving investors ruined. About 6,000 banks failed, and people stopped spending. The Wall Street Crash of October 29, 1929, plunged the United States into an economic depression from which it took 10 years to recover.

Words that changed the world

In The Grapes of Wrath, *Ma Joad says that the one thing she has learned, and continues to learn each day, is that if you are in trouble, are hurt, or need something, the only people you can turn to for help are poor people.*

Exploring the text

Ma Joad is a strong woman who holds her family together as they face hard times during the Great Depression. She advises that only the poor will help those who are struggling. Steinbeck believed that the only thing that kept many families going was the kindness of other people in the same situation as themselves. They shared the little they had. Some people had lost all their savings when the stock market crashed. As people stopped buying goods, firms went out of business and people lost their jobs. When their money ran out, they lost their homes. With no work to be had, families went hungry. The government gave them no help, so they had to rely on other people to help them.

A family with all its possessions on a trailer behind the car takes a break on its journey.

HISTORY'S STORY

Many Americans were suspicious of Steinbeck because he was a socialist. He believed society should give more support to workers and the poor. Steinbeck visited the communist Soviet Union in 1947 as a journalist. The Federal Bureau of Investigation (FBI) investigated him from the early 1940s, but Steinbeck never joined a communist or socialist party.

15

THE NEW DEAL

The worst years of the Great Depression were in 1932 and 1933. The president, Herbert Hoover, had told Americans that the economy was going to recover. Everyone could see that things were getting worse, but Hoover seemed to ignore this. During the 1932 presidential election, the Democratic candidate Franklin D. Roosevelt promised to change things to make the situation better. He said, "I pledge [promise] you, I pledge myself, to a new deal for the American people."

Franklin D. Roosevelt was the only president to serve more than two terms.

Roosevelt's promise caught the nation's attention, and he won the election easily. He said the country had gotten into a mess because the federal government had not been involved in the economy. Roosevelt believed that government should take control of all necessary aspects of life to help the country recover.

Creating work

As soon as he took office in March 1933, Roosevelt started a series of programs, or schemes, to get America working again. Named the "New Deal" for his popular pledge, the programs set up agencies and programs to create jobs. The Works Progress Administration (WPA), for example, created construction jobs by funding public works.

WPA workers built new roads, airports, schools, community buildings, public theaters, and libraries. Many of the buildings are still in use today. The Civilian Conservation Corps (CCC) gave jobs to young men who did conservation work, such as planting trees and fighting forest fires. The CCC alone employed around 3 million people for such tasks.

CCC workers enjoy a meal in the open air. They worked to preserve the landscape.

Relief, recovery, and reform

Roosevelt's programs had three main aims, which he called relief, recovery, and reform. By relief, he meant giving people jobs so they could earn money again, relieving them from poverty. Recovery meant the rebuilding of a strong U.S. economy with a modern infrastructure. Reform was achieved by a series of measures that were intended to make sure that an event like the Great Depression could not happen again. One of these reforms, for example, was the creation of the Federal Deposit Insurance Corporation (FDIC). In the future, the FDIC paid out money to people if their banks failed. Another reform was the introduction of Social Security. It was started to give money to the retired or disabled who could not earn their own money.

Many of the reforms were very successful. The economy slowly started to improve and there was a new optimism in many parts of the country, particularly in the cities. In the countryside, it was harder to change things. Large areas of farming land had been destroyed by a combination of overfarming and drought.

ON THE MOVE

A poster for one of the new government agencies

At one time, the plains in the heartland of North America were some of the most fertile grassland in the world. When settlers arrived in the Midwest in the mid-1800s, they farmed the land intensively. Within four generations, the land became overfarmed and infertile. The problem was made worse by a long drought that turned the soil to dry dust. Farmers were unable to grow crops and feed their families.

Heading west

More than 1 million farmers packed up their few possessions, abandoned their farms, and headed west to California in search of work and new land to farm. At first, it was usually the father of the family who left for California, but as times grew tougher, whole families moved in the hopes of a better future. They were known as "Okies" for Oklahoma, where many of them came from. They headed to the fertile Central Valley that John Steinbeck knew so well. Their dreams of starting their own farms were short-lived. With no vacant land for them to buy or lease, they became migrant workers who moved from farm to farm. In exchange for working in the fields, they were given a bed, food, and a small wage. Once the work was done, they moved on.

During the early part of the twentieth century, drought became an increasingly serious problem in the Midwest. By 1930, rain had stopped falling completely across Colorado, Kansas, Oklahoma, and Texas. About 100 million acres (40.4 million ha) of farmland across the four states was ruined by a combination of drought and high winds that whipped the bone-dry topsoil into the air. This disaster became known as the "Dust Bowl."

Words that changed the world

In The Grapes of Wrath, *Steinbeck describes houses that have windows and doors shut tight and wedged with cloth to keep out the dust. Despite this, the dust still manages to find its way inside and settles on tables, chairs, and dishes.*

This farmer's land has turned to dust.

HISTORY'S STORY

Dust from the Midwest formed huge clouds that turned everything dark and made breathing hard. One cloud rose 10,000 feet (3,000 m) into the air. In 1934, dust storms grew so big they reached Boston, New York City, and Chicago. They disrupted ships sailing along the East Coast. Dust got everywhere. In order to breathe, people had to cover their mouths and noses.

TIMELINE OF THE GREAT DEPRESSION

1929 U.S. unemployment reaches 3.1 percent.

1930 March: President Herbert Hoover says the worst of the Depression is over.

1930 Unemployment reaches 8.6 percent.

1931 February: Food riots break out.
Unemployment reaches 15.8 percent.
December: The Bank of the United States collapses.
Customers lose $200 million in deposits. It is the largest bank failure to date.

1932 Unemployment is 23.53 percent.

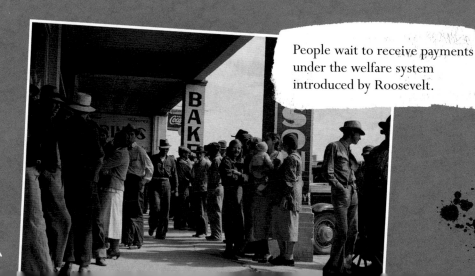

People wait to receive payments under the welfare system introduced by Roosevelt.

This memorial to Roosevelt shows men standing in line at a soup kitchen, a place that gave free food to the poor.

1932 November 8: Franklin D. Roosevelt is elected president on his promise of a "New Deal."

1933 March 9: The Emergency Banking Act is introduced to prevent bank collapses.

1933 Unemployment reaches its peak at 24.75 percent.

1934 Unemployment falls to 21.6 percent.

1935 Unemployment falls to 20.1 percent.

1936 Unemployment falls to 16.8 percent. November 3: Roosevelt is reelected as president for a second term.

1937 Unemployment is 14.18 percent.

1938 Unemployment rises again to 18.9 percent.

1939 Unemployment falls to 17.05 percent. September 3: World War II begins in Europe. Providing equipment for the war increases employment in the United States.

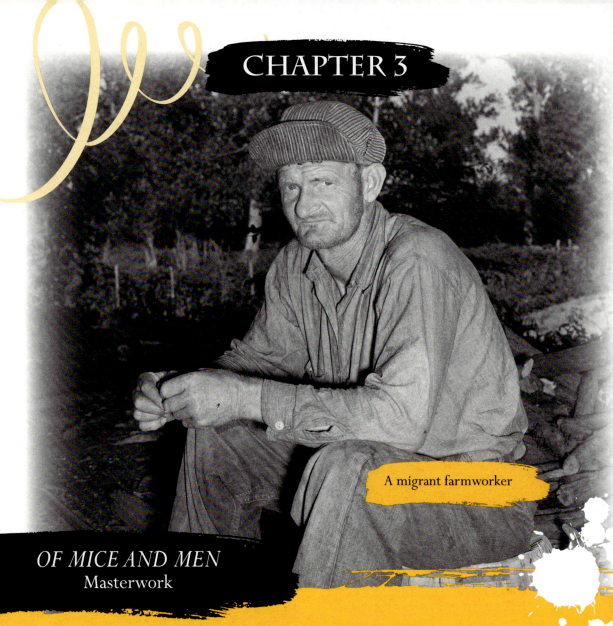

CHAPTER 3

A migrant farmworker

OF MICE AND MEN
Masterwork

Key characters in the book include:

George: a smart migrant worker, a friend of Lennie

Lennie: a migrant worker who likes to stroke soft things and has an intellectual disability

Candy: an old, one-handed ranch hand

Crooks: an African American stable hand

Curley: the boss's small, mean son

Curley's wife: a lonely woman who hates the ranch

Migrants George and Lennie work on a ranch as they dream of finding a farm of their own. George has always saved Lennie from trouble. When Lennie gets into trouble with the boss's daughter-in-law, helping him is not so simple.

The CHARACTERS in *Of Mice and Men* DREAM of a better future and WORK tirelessly on the LAND. But despite their HOPES and STRUGGLES, TRAGEDY follows the characters and the tale is one of DESPAIR rather than SALVATION.

INSPIRATIONS

John Steinbeck spent six years at Stanford University, where he studied English literature on and off before dropping out. In order to pay for his classes, he spent his breaks working on ranches in the Salinas Valley, where *Of Mice and Men* is set.

At the time, the valley was known as the "salad bowl of the nation." Refrigerated railroad cars transported lettuce, or "green gold," to the cities of the east. The fertile 50-mile-long (80 km) valley had been home to generations of farmers and ranchers. In the nineteenth century, they had grown wheat, barley, and sugar beet, but by the early twentieth century they had switched to vegetables and lettuce.

… he spent his breaks working on raches in the Salinas Valley …

Steinbeck saw the other side of the valley's success. He saw workers failing to achieve their dreams and being left lonely and disappointed. Steinbeck heard many different stories from the workers he met. He knew that one day he would turn their tales into a work of fiction.

Steinbeck worked on farms to pay for his studies at Stanford University.

Most of the farmland in California is owned by businesses that farm on a huge scale.

Words that changed the world

In Of Mice and Men, *George tells Lennie that ranch workers are the loneliest people in the world because they have no family and no home. They just travel to a ranch to earn money, then waste it in a nearby town. George says the ranchers have nothing to look forward to.*

Exploring the text

George is trying to reassure his friend Lennie that life is going to work out for them. George describes the lives of most migrant farmhands, who move from job to job and who live for their paychecks. George has convinced Lennie that their story will be different. Whatever the problems, they will manage to achieve their dream of owning their own piece of land. George convinces Lennie that the situation in which they find themselves working as migrant laborers is only temporary. Lennie, who has the intelligence of a young child, believes completely in George's vision of their future. He makes George repeat the details of this future over and over to comfort him.

WRITING
OF MICE OF MEN

By the time Steinbeck published *Of Mice and Men* in 1937, he was already a successful writer. He had hit the big time with his 1935 comic novel *Tortilla Flat*. Now he set out to write a novella—a story that was shorter than a usual novel—that could also be turned into a stage play. Steinbeck set himself a maximum of 30,000 words to tell his story. He already knew the subject matter would be close to his heart. He wanted to illustrate the themes of loneliness and disappointed dreams by using characters based on the people he had met on ranches in the Salinas Valley.

Workers remove weeds from beds of guayule in California. Guayule is a plant that provides a source of rubber.

Steinbeck was fascinated by the way that people's dreams could survive even in the face of difficulties. There was so much that could go wrong for the people he worked alongside. By the time *Of Mice and Men* was published, the Great Depression and the Dust Bowl had provided harsh reminders that disaster was never far away.

Steinbeck wrote the novella with a lot of dialogue, so it was straightforward to turn it into a script. However, the play was a flop when it was performed in San Francisco shortly after the book was published. A new version of the play, with a revised script by George Kaufmann, opened in New York a few months later. This time, it was a hit. Steinbeck refused to travel from California to watch the play, however. He claimed the script was perfect in his mind, so any staging was bound to be a disappointment.

The eighteenth-century poet Robert Burns inspired the title *Of Mice and Men*.

HISTORY'S STORY

The title *Of Mice and Men* is taken from a poem by the Scottish poet Robert Burns called "To a Mouse." It says, "The best laid schemes o' mice and men / Gang aft a-gley / An' leave us naught but grief an' pain / For promised joy." The poem tells how the mouse's home in the field is destroyed by a plow. Burns suggests our best plans to achieve "joy" often go wrong—"gang aft a-gley," in Scots dialect.

PLOT BREAKDOWN

Of Mice and Men tells the story of two friends, George and Lennie. They arrive in Soledad as they travel through California. They are on the run because Lennie has been falsely accused of attacking a young woman. They are looking for work, but hope one day to have enough money to own some land of their own. They get jobs on a ranch but soon run into problems. The boss's son, Curley, picks on Lennie, but it is soon clear that George will defend Lennie no matter what. Curley's wife is unhappy and she flirts with Lennie.

The other ranch hands are nicer than Curley. George and Lennie make friends with Candy, who has lost his hand in an accident. The three agree to buy a piece of land together when they have finished working on the ranch. Candy's dog is deliberately shot and killed by a mean worker named Carlson. Another ranch hand, Slim, gives Lennie and Candy a puppy to replace the old dog.

These workers are loading crates of lettuce onto a truck on a farm in the Salinas Valley.

Lennie is left alone

Things seem to be going well, so George leaves Lennie while he goes into town with the other hands. While he is away, Lennie makes friends with Crooks, who is picked on by the other workers because he is African American. Curley's wife tries to flirt with the men, but when this goes wrong she threatens Crooks with being lynched, or killed.

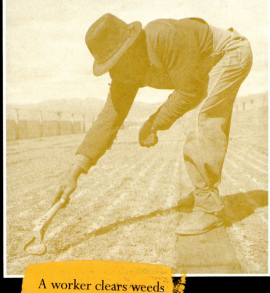

A worker clears weeds from planted soil.

The next day, Lennie accidentally kills his puppy while he is stroking it because he does not realize his own strength. Curley's wife is lonely. She tells Lennie he can stroke her hair, but when she feels just how strong his hands are, she starts to scream. Lennie panics and accidentally breaks her neck, killing her. Lennie runs away. The other ranch hands find the woman's body and George instantly realizes what has happened. Curley vows to get revenge for his dead wife.

A tragic ending

George finds Lennie in the hiding place the two had agreed upon for Lennie. If the others find Lennie, George worries, they will kill him slowly and painfully. George comforts Lennie by telling him again the story of how they will one day have their own ranch, even though he now knows the dream will never come true. As he tells the story, he shoots Lennie from behind, killing him. When the other ranch hands arrive, Curley and Carlson are angry not to be able to kill Lennie themselves, but Slim comforts George. He tells him he had no choice but to kill his friend.

MAIN CHARACTERS IN *OF MICE AND MEN*

A migrant worker

Lennie

A large but childlike man whose strength makes him a good worker but which also leads to disaster. He is reliant on George to care for him. He likes stroking anything soft, such as fur or hair.

George

Travels with and takes care of Lennie. He promises Lennie they will have a better future. George finds them both work on the ranch, which ultimately leads to Lennie killing Curley's wife. To save Lennie from a worse death, George shoots his best friend.

Candy

A worker on the ranch who worries about his future because he has lost a hand in an accident. He offers Lennie and George money to help buy a farm so he can live with them in the future. His old dog is shot dead by Carlson.

Crooks

An African American stable hand who has been discriminated against. He makes friends with Lennie.

Curley

A short, mean man who is the boss's son. He is jealous of any man who is nice to his wife. Curley picks fights with anyone bigger than him.

Curley's wife

A bored housewife who dreams of leaving the ranch and becoming an actress. She flirts with the ranch hands but ends up paying with her life.

Slim

The only figure in the book who seems happy with his life. The others turn to him for advice. He comforts George after George kills Lennie.

The Boss

The rancher only appears once and is never named.

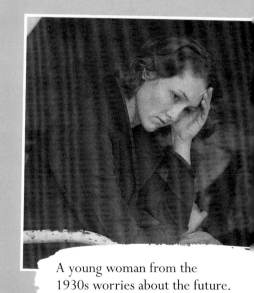

This photograph is entitled *Migrant Mother*.

A young woman from the 1930s worries about the future.

CHAPTER 4

Animals are important companions in *Of Mice and Men*.

OF MICE AND MEN
Key Themes

Key themes in the book include:

Loneliness and isolation

Prejudice

Dreams and aspirations

Destiny

Death

Companionship

Poverty

Oppression

Steinbeck's writing is BRAVE. It does not TURN AWAY from the terrible SADNESS and HARDSHIP experienced by people. Instead, it DELVES into the UNCOMFORTABLE issues of LONELINESS and PREJUDICE along with POVERTY and DEATH.

DREAMS AND ASPIRATIONS

Curley's wife dreams of being a famous movie star, like Mae West (above).

All the characters in *Of Mice and Men* once had dreams and aspirations, or hopes. The reader can see that none of the men or Curley's wife will achieve their dreams. George and Lennie share a dream of a better life where they own their own land. Whether George really believes in the dream is unclear. Sometimes, it seems he actually does believe things will end well for him and Lennie. At other times, however, it seems as though he is just telling the story in order to convince Lennie and keep his friend happy.

Candy buys into George and Lennie's dream, but he knows it will never happen. Crooks has had all his hopes and dreams taken away, partly because of the color of his skin. Two more ranch hands, Whit and Carlson, have become used to living without any hopes for a better future.

George and Lennie share a dream of a better life ...

Curley's wife dreams of being a movie star, but it is clear that will never happen while she lives on the ranch. Curley is the only character who appears to be living the dream. He has a wife and will one day inherit the ranch. In fact, however, his life is just as bad as those of the other characters. Curley is a bully whom nobody likes, including his own wife.

Words that changed the world

In Of Mice and Men, George often tells Lennie a story about how their lives will get better. He says they will get enough money to buy a small house, some land, and pigs. Lennie is so excited by the tale that he joins in, shouting that they will even have rabbits!

Exploring the text

In George's story, he and Lennie will one day achieve their dream of owning land, a small house, and animals. George repeats the story whenever Lennie becomes upset. Steinbeck suggests that George knows that the dream will never come true but Lennie believes in it. For Lennie, life would be perfect with the addition of rabbits to stroke. The men's dream is no different from the dreams of millions of people. Unlike Curley's wife's dream of becoming a movie star, it does not seem impossible—but in the end, it proves just as impossible. Many of the characters in the book do not live in the present. They are always dreaming of a better future.

Every time George describes the farm they will have, Lennie reminds him they must have rabbits to stroke.

POVERTY AND OPPRESSION

Of Mice and Men is set against the background of the Great Depression and the Dust Bowl, when farmworkers moved west to look for work. George and Lennie are looking for a ranch where they can work, sleep, and earn some money. None of the characters in the book have enough money to lead the lives they want. It seems that Curley is an exception, because he will one day inherit the ranch, but Steinbeck shows that Curley, too, is not leading the life he wants.

The farmhands are locked into a cycle. They earn just enough money to live and perhaps enjoy themselves for a night out, but not enough to save for the future. They have reduced their lives to a few needs.

The men in Steinbeck's novel have no way to reach their dream of owning a house like this one.

The lack of any chance to save money means that workers such as George, Lennie, Candy, Crooks, and Slim have to rely on their work at the ranch. If they lose their jobs, they have no way to live. Curley uses this as a threat to make the men do as they are told.

President Roosevelt signs the Social Security Act into law on August 14, 1935.

Help from the government

One reason there was so much suffering in the Great Depression was that there was no help for the unemployed. People relied on their relatives and friends to survive. One of the reforms President Roosevelt introduced was a welfare system, in which the government provided help for the poorest people in society. The Social Security Act of 1935 set up a system of payments from the federal government to help the unemployed and the retired. The new welfare system provided money to support workers who could not earn enough money for their families to live on. Instead of having to rely on friends and family, people could now ask the government to help them.

HISTORY'S STORY

The idea of welfare systems was not a new one. Economists believed a social security system introduced in the 1880s had helped Germany to industrialize more quickly than it would have done otherwise. Roosevelt hoped his new welfare system would do the same for the United States, while also helping the millions of people affected by both the Great Depression and the effects of the Dust Bowl.

COMPANIONSHIP AND LONELINESS

At the heart of the novella is the friendship between George and Lennie. Despite the two men's intense loyalty to each other, however, John Steinbeck provides many clues in the book to show that he is writing about loneliness as much as companionship.

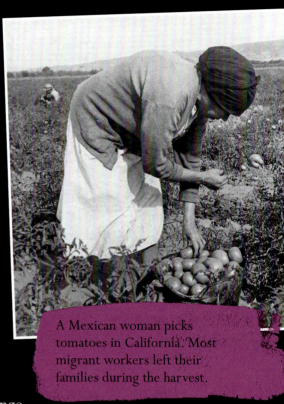

A Mexican woman picks tomatoes in California. Most migrant workers left their families during the harvest.

The nearest town to the ranch is called Soledad, which means "solitude" or "loneliness" in Spanish. The men who live on the ranch are all loners. None of them have any friends, and they find it strange that George and Lennie are so close. The ranch hands go to town on Saturday nights, but even when they are partying together, they are still isolated from one another and lonely. Curley and his wife are married, but they are both still lonely. Curley's wife tries to overcome her loneliness by flirting with the ranch hands. Even George, who is devoted to Lennie, at one point in the novel claims that he has no family.

Finding companions

Everyone in the story is looking for a companion. Animals provide companionship, but Lennie kills any animal he has because of his own strength. When Candy's old dog is killed by Carlson, it leaves him with nothing. Curley's wife's flirtation with the ranch hands ends in disaster after Lennie kills her. Crooks lives alone because he is African American and is discriminated against. When Lennie visits him, Crooks is so used to being alone that he does not enjoy company.

George and Lennie are opposites. They have grown used to each other, however, and both understand that without each other life would be even more lonely. After George kills Lennie, he is left alone. Steinbeck does not give the reader any hope that his characters will become less lonely or more happy.

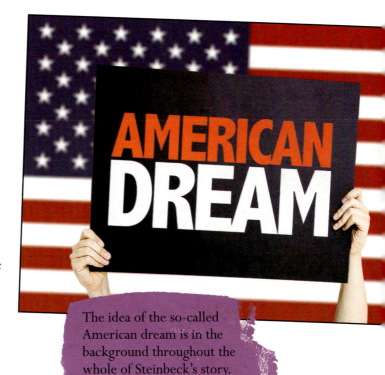

The idea of the so-called American dream is in the background throughout the whole of Steinbeck's story.

HISTORY'S STORY

In 1931, writer James Truslow Adams coined the phrase "the American dream." He said the United States was a country where anything was possible if you worked hard. Adams said Americans believed that the ideals of freedom, equality, and opportunity are available to everyone. Happiness and material comfort are the reward for a life of hard work. Steinbeck shows that this is not the reality.

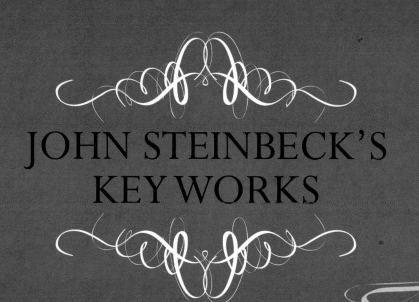

JOHN STEINBECK'S KEY WORKS

Tortilla Flat (1935)
This novel was Steinbeck's first study of migrant Mexican workers in the Salinas Valley.

The Grapes of Wrath (1939)
Steinbeck's most famous novel describes the effects of the Great Depression and the Dust Bowl on farmers. It describes terrible migrant labor camps in California.

The Log from the Sea of Cortez (1941)
This nonfiction account introduces the reader to Steinbeck's interest in ecology and his holistic approach to life, as influenced by his co-author, Ed Ricketts.

Many of Steinbeck's books are set in the Salinas Valley.

A cannery on Ocean View Avenue in Monterey

Cannery Row (1945)

A comic novel about the lives of those who worked in the fishing industry along Monterey's Ocean View Avenue. The novel was so popular that in 1958 Ocean View Avenue was renamed Cannery Row.

East of Eden (1952)

Set in the Salinas Valley, this novel is a retelling of the story of Cain and Abel in the Bible and of good versus evil.

The Winter of Our Discontent (1961)

Steinbeck studies the decline in morality in the United States in a story about one man's moral dilemma. The book won him the Nobel Prize for Literature in 1962.

Travels with Charley: In Search of America (1962)

Steinbeck travels around America with his dog, Charley, to rediscover a country he feels he no longer knows.

CHAPTER 5

Steinbeck and his third wife, Elaine

RIGHTS FOR ALL
Effecting Change

Steinbeck's later career:

1939: Publishes *The Grapes of Wrath*

1940: Awarded the Pulitzer Prize for Fiction

1943: Is divorced from Carol, his first wife

1943: Marries Gwyn, his second wife

1944: Thomas Steinbeck is born

1945: Publishes *Cannery Row*

1946: John Steinbeck IV is born

1948: Is divorced from Gwyn

1950: Marries Elaine

1952: Publishes *East of Eden*

1962: Wins the Nobel Prize for Literature

1968: Dies on December 20, in New York City

Steinbeck said that his motivation for writing *East of Eden* was to show his sons what LIFE was like in the COUNTRY where he GREW UP. He wanted to SPEAK DIRECTLY to them and OTHER READERS through his WRITING.

A CONTINUING CAMPAIGN

In 1939, Steinbeck published *The Grapes of Wrath*, which many people consider one of the greatest epic novels of American literature. The novel tells the story of the Joads, a family of poor tenant farmers who are driven from Oklahoma. The continuing drought and the effects of the Dust Bowl have made their land impossible to farm. Like millions of others, the Joads head to California, where they hope a brighter future lies. Along the way, they hear stories that life is just as hard in California, too.

… the Joads head to California, where they hope a brighter future lies.

In California, the Joads are forced to live in terrible conditions in a migrant camp with thousands of other workers. They see how the large farms exploit the workers. Trapped by their poverty, the family tries to make the best of an awful situation by helping others. Steinbeck had visited migrant camps and he wanted the world to know how terrible the conditions were. He wanted his readers to see the results of man's inhumanity to man. He set out to show the reverse. If people are kind to their fellow human beings, life is much better for everyone.

A family lives in a shelter next to their car in a migrant camp in California.

Words that changed the world

In The Grapes of Wrath, *the Joads meet a farmer who is on his way home because there is no fertile land left in the West. The farmer tells the Joads that people there are terrified of one another because they know that when a person is hungry, they will do anything to get food—even if that means taking another person's land.*

Exploring the text

The farmer explains that people have turned against one another. Farmers who own land are terrified that desperate people will take it. They do not dare leave their land fallow, or unplanted, in case someone else starts growing crops there. Fallow land is a sin, says the farmer. In fact, soil has to be left fallow after growing crops to recover its fertility. Steinbeck believed people had a duty to help one another. The farmer's words reflect his belief that when life is reduced to fear and suspicion, everything falls apart.

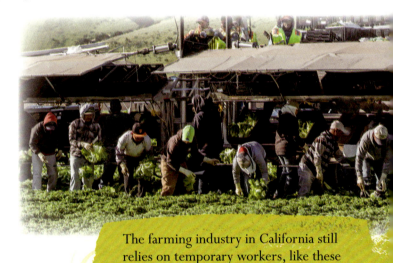

The farming industry in California still relies on temporary workers, like these people who are harvesting lettuce.

HISTORY'S STORY

In some ways the treatment of migrant workers in California has changed little from Steinbeck's day. Hundreds of thousands of temporary workers pick fruit and vegetables. By paying them low wages, farmers are able to sell their produce at lower prices. This is good for shoppers, but leaves the migrant workers trapped in a hand-to-mouth existence from which they cannot break free.

HAVES AND HAVE-NOTS

The United States joined World War II after its fleet was bombed by the Japanese at Pearl Harbor in 1941.

By the end of the 1930s, the policies of the New Deal had started to work. The worst effects of the Great Depression gradually began to pass. It was not until World War II that better employment rates returned again and the Great Depression finally ended.

When the stock market crashed on October 29, 1929, many Americans believed it was a temporary blip. They included the president, Herbert Hoover. When the market recovered some ground, Hoover announced in March 1930 that the worst had passed. He was completely wrong. Between 1930 and 1933, unemployment continued to rise. At its peak in 1933, 24.9 percent of Americans were unemployed—one in four of all workers.

A welfare system

When Franklin D. Roosevelt became president in 1932, he promised a new way of dealing with the effects of the Great Depression. At the heart of his plan was greater involvement in people's lives by the federal government, including the creation of a welfare system.

The Social Security Act became law in August 1935. To begin with, the government provided the money paid out to elderly Americans each month. Starting in January 1937, however, the money was raised from working people in the form of social security taxes. The idea was that this money would be used to help all Americans who did not have enough money to cover their basic needs, along with senior citizens.

The welfare system was designed to help families whose income was not enough to live comfortably.

The first retirement benefits check was paid in January 1940. Since then, what is now known as the U.S. Social Security Administration (SSA) has grown into a multibillion-dollar agency. In 2010, more than 54 million Americans received $712 billion in social security benefits. As well as helping retired Americans, the system is now a vital part of the health care system. Millions of Americans still rely on Medicare and Medicaid, which have their roots in the New Deal welfare system, to help pay their medical bills.

War ends the Great Depression

The aim of the New Deal was to help Americans either directly with financial assistance or by creating jobs that would enable them to support themselves. It was broadly successful in helping to lessen the effects of the Great Depression, but it was not until the United States went to war that the economy fully recovered. The need for equipment to arm U.S., British, and Soviet military forces meant that there was suddenly work available for many more people. Higher employment rates returned to the United States by 1942.

PEOPLE AND LANDSCAPES

John Steinbeck was a pioneer of a holistic approach to the environment that is now very fashionable. Growing up in the Salinas Valley, Steinbeck witnessed firsthand how big business destroyed the landscape he loved so much with intensive farming. In his novels, it is the migrant workers who toil in the fields, wearing out their bodies. Meanwhile, the landowners are far away poring over their account books to see how best to make a profit.

The Dust Bowl was caused by a combination of a natural drought and human overfarming of the land.

A biologist friend

During the summer of 1923, Steinbeck took a biology course at Hopkins Marine Station in Pacific Grove, California. There, he studied the work of the U.S. biologist William Emerson Ritter. Ritter believed in organicism, which is the idea that everything in nature is part of an organic whole. Ritter argued that all living things were interdependent and were connected in a vast, complex web. Steinbeck embraced Ritter's theory, and used his novels to show what happens when the complex web is disturbed.

Humans and nature

For Steinbeck, the Dust Bowl of the 1930s was proof that humans were out of step with nature. The destruction of the fertile grasslands of the plains in just four generations was proof that Americans had put short-term profit above any long-term concern for the environment. Steinbeck also understood that, for many farmers, being removed from the land was like being isolated from their fellow humans.

In Steinbeck's mind the natural world was always "magical" and "special." Steinbeck believed there were two American landscapes. One was the physical landscape he could see, while the other was his own interior landscape, which was shaped by the places he had experienced. He was shaped by the Salinas Valley, which is the background of many of his novels. He looked back on the valley during his childhood as a paradise that had been destroyed by the arrival of large farms.

Steinbeck and Ed Ricketts sailed around the Gulf of Mexico, studying its systems of marine life.

HISTORY'S STORY

One of Steinbeck's most important relationships was with his friend and mentor Ed Ricketts, the marine biologist. Like Ricketts, Steinbeck believed humans had to share Earth with all other living organisms. He and Ricketts spent six weeks in 1940 exploring the marine life of the Gulf of California, also known as the Sea of Cortez. Their record of their trip, *The Log from the Sea of Cortez* (1941), was a unique combination of literature and biological writing.

49

RECORDING THE GREAT DEPRESSION

John Steinbeck was one of a number of writers, artists, and photographers who recorded the effects of the Great Depression on the United States.

Dorothea Lange (1895–1965)

A photographer and photojournalist who photographed the human cost of the Depression. Her most famous photograph was *Migrant Mother* (1936; see page 31).

Martha Gellhorn (1908–1998)

A novelist who worked as an investigator reporting on the impact of the Depression, which she published in her collection of stories, *The Trouble I've Seen* (1936).

Walker Evans (1903–1975)

A photographer and photojournalist who documented the effects of the Depression.

This is a portrait of photographer Walker Evans.

Martha Gellhorn and her husband, Ernest Hemingway, visit China in 1941.

John Dos Passos (1896–1970)

A novelist who had studied socialism in Russia. Dos Passos believed there were two Americas—one rich, one poor—which he documented in his *USA* trilogy: *The 42nd Parallel* (1930), *1919* (1932), and *The Big Money* (1936).

Edward Hopper (1882–1967)

An artist who painted his vision of life during the Depression.

Photographer Dorothea Lange traveled the country to record the Great Depression.

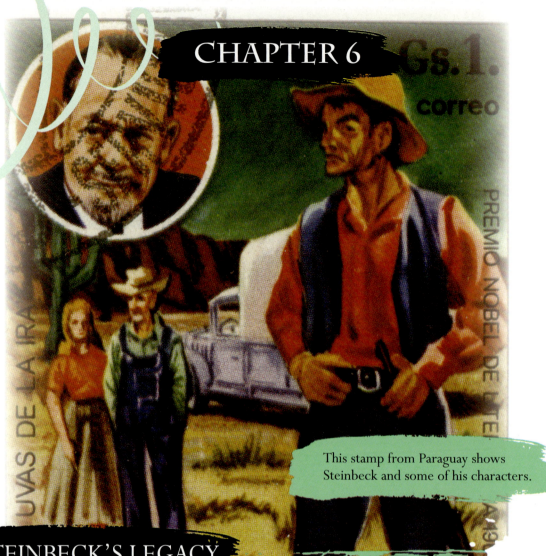

CHAPTER 6

This stamp from Paraguay shows Steinbeck and some of his characters.

STEINBECK'S LEGACY
Aftermath

Comparing past with present:

1929: 136,000 farms in California

2007: 81,000 farms in California

1929: 332,000 farmworkers

1997: 260,000 farmworkers

1930: 13.3 percent people employed in Californian farms out of total workforce

2010: 2.3 percent people employed in Californian farms out of total workforce

The tractor is described as being a MACHINE that could both TURN the LAND and turn PEOPLE off the land. Steinbeck said that a tractor was not very different from a TANK because people could be FRIGHTENED and HURT by both.

FINAL
ASSESSMENT

In 1962, Steinbeck won the Nobel Prize for Literature, the leading literary prize in the world. The award confirmed his position as one of the great chroniclers of twentieth-century America. Since Steinbeck had written *Of Mice and Men* in 1937, he had published some of the most popular books in American literature, including *The Grapes of Wrath* (1939), *Cannery Row* (1945), and *East of Eden* (1952). He had also turned his attention to the changes taking place in his country.

In 1961, Steinbeck published the novel that won him the Nobel Prize. *The Winter of Our Discontent* tells the story of the moral decline of the novel's main character, Ethan, as he lies and cheats his way to riches. For Steinbeck, Ethan's behavior parallels the moral decline the writer saw going on around him in the United States.

He had also turned his attention to the changes taking place …

Steinbeck gave an acceptance speech when he received the Nobel Prize in December 1962. He explained what he saw as the writer's role: to show human dreams along with human failures. Steinbeck stated that a writer is "delegated to declare" mankind's capacity for courage, compassion, and love.

Words that changed the world

In Travels with Charley, *Steinbeck describes his journey as being like a meal of many courses served to a starving man. At first, the man will try to eat everything, but will then find that he needs to show restraint if he wants to keep his appetite for the food.*

Exploring the text

Toward the end of *Travels with Charley*, Steinbeck is on his way home to California after a road trip of about 10,000 miles (16,000 km) across the United States in 1960. Steinbeck had set out to answer the question, "What are Americans like today?" He soon realized that the country he thought he knew had changed. He also realized that he was concerned about the nature of the country he discovered. However, he also realized that it was impossible for one man to grasp all aspects of the nation in a single journey.

Steinbeck and Charley traveled in *Rocinante*, a pickup truck with a miniature camper.

HISTORY'S STORY

To accompany him on his road trip, Steinbeck took along his old French poodle, Charley. The writer talked to Charley as if the dog were a person, and he frequently records asking Charley's opinion about what to do next. If anybody tried to address Charley in baby talk, both Steinbeck and the dog avoided that person!

MIGRANT WORKERS

The issues that Steinbeck raised in *Of Mice and Men* and *The Grapes of Wrath* about the treatment of migrant farm workers are still relevant today. In Steinbeck's day, most of the workers in California came from other U.S. states. Today, Mexico is the biggest source of such labor. Mexicans have largely replaced American migrant workers in the fields.

Hard work

Picking fruit and vegetables is hard, back-breaking work, which historically has been poorly paid. Many Americans do not want the jobs, as pickers work from 10 to 12 hours a day, six days a week. For the Mexicans who make up 90 percent of California's farmworkers, however, the work pays much better than any job they are likely to get in Mexico. The average picker in California earned $15,000 in 2014. During the harvest, pickers are paid for each box of produce they fill, so the longer, harder, and quicker they work, the more money they are able to make.

Many Mexican workers travel to the United States for the higher wages there.

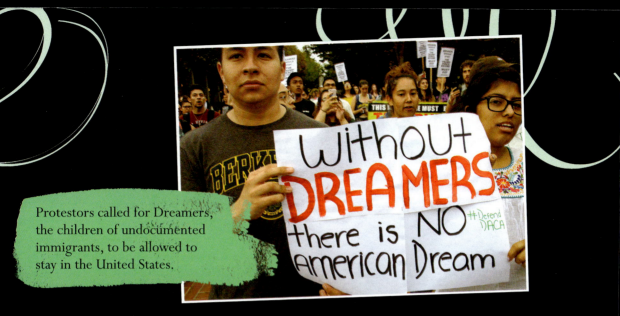

Protestors called for Dreamers, the children of undocumented immigrants, to be allowed to stay in the United States.

Undocumented immigrants

Up to half of the Mexican pickers in California are undocumented immigrants. Many come to California each year just to work on the harvest. However, between 2000 and 2014, those workers fell from 25 percent to 2 percent of the migrant workforce. Over recent years, the number of Mexican workers has fallen even further as a result of tighter U.S. immigration policy and increased border security. In addition, the economy in Mexico is also improving. That makes the task of crossing the border for work less attractive.

Immigration—both legal and illegal—continues to be a subject of intense debate in the United States. For the farm owners in California, the question is crucial. In 2017, more Mexican workers were leaving the United States than were arriving. That same year, a shortage of migrant workers led to crops rotting in the fields in California before they could be picked. As a result, farmers lost money and agricultural businesses have seen their incomes fall dramatically. The lack of pickers means that farmers have had to raise wages to attract workers. This, in turn, has led to price increases for Californian crops—which in turn affects every household in the United States.

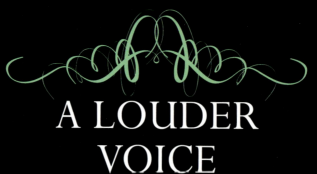

A LOUDER VOICE

John Steinbeck's description of the Great Depression and the Dust Bowl has never been bettered. Many writers since have followed Steinbeck's example, however. They have written about Steinbeck's favorite subjects—the American landscape, poverty, inequality, and the dispossessed.

Contemporary writers such as Annie Proulx write about the landscapes of Wyoming and Texas, and the effect they have on the people who live there. Like Steinbeck, Joan Didion was from California. She wrote about the impact of the state not just on herself but on the whole of the United States in the 1960s. In *The Road* (2006), Cormac McCarthy described America after a huge disaster in which the landscape has been destroyed and all social order has broken down. Junot Diaz, a Dominican-American writer, describes poverty in the Dominican communities of East Coast cities.

This view from an airplane shows how California's valleys have been turned into farmland.

These writers do not just write about what it is like to be American. They explore what it is like to come from a very particular landscape or community. They explore the idea of place in the same way Steinbeck explored the Salinas Valley of California.

A challenged reputation

Today, John Steinbeck's novels are seen as being among the greatest works of American literature. However, they have often been controversial. The Board of Supervisors in Kern County, California, banned *The Grapes of Wrath* because they did not like Steinbeck's depiction of the county as a corrupt place where people were exploited. Landowners called the book "communist propaganda" and arranged for copies of the novel to be burned in Bakersfield, California. The Kansas City Board of Education banned the book on the grounds that it was immoral.

Steinbeck's views have been so unpopular they have, at times, led to his books being burned.

Of Mice and Men has also been frequently challenged and banned since it was published in 1937. It has been attacked because of its swearing; its themes; its treatment of disability, women, and African Americans; and its violence. Despite this criticism, it remains one of the best-loved stories of the twentieth century.

HISTORY'S STORY

In 1974, *Of Mice and Men* was banned in Syracuse, Indiana, and three years later in Oil City, Pennsylvania. In Knoxville, Tennessee, the book was removed from public schools as a "filthy" book that contained swearing. The most recent challenge to the novella was in 2014 in Minnesota, when two parents complained about its use of "Jesus Christ" as a swear word. The challenge was rejected by the courts.

MAJOR MOVIE AND STAGE ADAPTATIONS OF STEINBECK'S WORK

Plays

Of Mice and Men: 1937, 1975, 2014

Tortilla Flat: 1938

The Moon Is Down: 1942

Burning Bright: 1950 (musical)

Pipe Dream: 1955 (musical based on *Sweet Thursday*)

Here's Where I Belong: 1968 (musical based on *East of Eden*)

The Grapes of Wrath: 1985, 1990

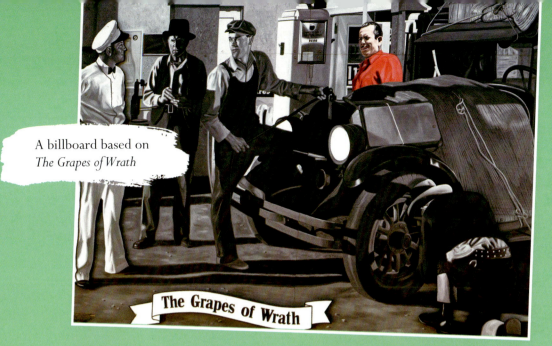

A billboard based on
The Grapes of Wrath

The Grapes of Wrath

Movies

1937	*Of Mice and Men*
1940	*The Grapes of Wrath*
1941	*The Forgotten Village*
1942	*Tortilla Flat*
1943	*The Moon Is Down*
1947	*The Pearl*
1949	*The Red Pony*
1952	*Viva Zapata!*
1955	*East of Eden*
1957	*The Wayward Bus*
1982	*Cannery Row*
1983	*The Winter of Our Discontent*
1992	*Of Mice and Men*
2016	*In Dubious Battle*

GLOSSARY

benefits payments to help people

biology the study of living things

boom a period of economic growth

cannery a factory where food is put into cans

communist believing the government should own everything and share it among everyone

companionship having friends for company

contemporary modern, of the present time

controversial causing disagreement

corrupt dishonest

debate an argument about a topic

delegated given a task

deposits payments of savings into a bank

destiny someone's future

dialogue conversation between people in a book

discriminated treated badly because of someone's race or religion

dispossessed people who have lost everything

drought a long period with little or no rain

economy the business, industry, and trade of a country

ecosystems networks of living things

environment natural surroundings

epic on a large, heroic scale

equality treating everyone the same

estate a large area of countryside

exploit to make use of people unfairly

fertile easily able to grow crops and other plants

fiction an imaginary story

flirts acts playfully as if attracted to someone

Great Depression a period of low economic activity and global poverty in the 1930s

hand-to-mouth meeting only current needs

harvest the period when ripe crops are picked

holistic including everything in a single system

homesick missing home while away

immigration the arrival of new people to live in a country

immoral wrong

income the money someone earns

industrialize to become dominated by industry

infertile unable to grow crops

infrastructure the structures needed for an economy, such as roads and power lines

inherit to receive property from someone when they die

intensively with concentration, thoroughly

investments money paid to buy shares in businesses in the hopes of making more money

loyalty strong support for another person

manual labor work done with the hands

marine biology the study of life in the sea

material related to physical things

mentor a friend and advisor

migrant workers people who move around to find work

moral concerned with right and wrong

opportunity a chance to succeed

oppression ill treatment of a group of people

optimism a good feeling about the future

overfarming growing so many crops that soil becomes exhausted

photojournalist a reporter who tells news stories through photographs

plains large areas of open grassland

poverty severe financial hardship

prejudice a dislike of someone based on preformed ideas rather than reality

profit money made after all costs have been paid

public works construction such as roads or schools carried out by the government

ranch hand a worker on a ranch

relevant meaningful

revenge harming someone in return for harm they have caused

script the text of a play or movie

socialist believing major industries should be owned and controlled by the government, rather than individuals

social security a system of payments for people who are unable to work

specimens animals collected to be studied

stable hand a worker who looks after horses

stalled halted

stock market a place where people buy and sell small parts of large businesses

topsoil the top layer of farmland

welfare maintaining the well-being of people in need

wrath anger

FOR MORE INFORMATION

BOOKS

McArthur, Debra. *John Steinbeck: The Grapes of Wrath and Of Mice and Men.* New York, NY: Marshall Cavendish Benchmark, 2009.

Morretta, Alison. *John Steinbeck and the Great Depression.* New York, NY: Cavendish Square Publishing, 2015.

Otfinoski, Steven. *The Great Depression.* New York, NY: Scholastic Inc., 2018.

Steinbeck, John. *Of Mice and Men.* New York, NY: Penguin Classics, 2006.

WEBSITES

Great Depression—
www.ducksters.com/history/us_1900s/great_depression.php
This page has a description of the causes and effects of the Great Depression.

His Works—www.steinbeck.org/about-john/his-works/
This interactive page features information on Steinbeck's many writings.

John Steinbeck—www.biography.com/people/john-steinbeck-9493358
This page offers an account of Steinbeck's life and works.

INDEX